THE HUMAN MACHINE

THE BRAIN AND NERVOUS SYSTEM

Richard Spilsbury

© 2008 Heinemann Library
a division of Reed Elsevier Inc.
Chicago, Illinois

Customer Service 888-454-2279
Visit our website at www.heinemannraintree.com

Designed by Victoria Bevan and AMR Design Ltd
Illustrations by Medi-mation
Picture Research by Hannah Taylor

Originated by Chroma
Printed and bound in China by CTPS

12 11 10 09 08
10 9 8 7 6 5 4 3 2 1

Library of Congress Cataloging-in-Publication Data
Spilsbury, Richard.

The brain and nervous system / Richard Spilsbury.
       p. cm. -- (The human machine)
   Includes index.
   ISBN-13: 978-1-4329-0903-1 (hardback : alk. paper)
   ISBN-13: 978-1-4329-0910-9 (pbk. : alk. paper)
  1. Nervous system--Juvenile literature. 2. Brain--Juvenile literature. I. Title.
   QP361.5.S65 2007
   612.8--dc22

                              2007031958

Acknowledgments
The publishers would like to thank the following for permission to reproduce photographs: ©Alamy pp. **9**, **14** (Aflo Foto Agency), **6** (Blend Images), **21** (Jeff Greenburg); ©Corbis pp. **8** (Royalty Free), **24** (Anna Clopet), **23** (Jocelyn Bain Hogg), **20** (Push Pictures), **5** (Will & Deni McIntyre); ©Getty Images pp. **26**, **17** (Digital Vision), **16** (Hola Images), **13** and **18** (Photodisc), **4** (Taxi), **15** (The Image Bank); ©iStockphoto p. **29** (Justin Horrocks); ©Photolibrary p. **27** (Image de Sud); ©Science Photo Library pp. **28** (Roger Harris), **11** (Sovereign, ISM), **25** (Steve Gschmeissner).

Cover photograph of the nervous system reproduced with permission of ©Science Photo Library/Pasieka.

The publishers would like to thank David Wright for his assistance in the preparation of this book.

Every effort has been made to contact copyright holders of any material reproduced in this book. Any omissions will be rectified in subsequent printings if notice is given to the publishers.

Contents

Any words appearing in the text in bold, **like this**, are explained in the glossary.

How Do We Control Our Bodies?

People ride bikes by controlling them. A pull on the handlebars changes direction. A press on the brakes slows the bike down. Pedaling harder makes it go faster. The human body is a bit like a living machine. Everything we do, including the way we grow, breathe, and move, is controlled by the nervous system.

The nervous system allows us to experience the world around us. It converts patterns of light and color into sights we can see. It transforms movements of air caused by vibrating objects into sounds we can hear. By using our nervous system, we can tell many things apart, including hot and cold, smooth and hard, and wet and dry.

Your nervous system lets you feel excited and frightened at an amusement park.

Nerve headquarters

The brain is the headquarters of the nervous system. It is like a powerful computer that processes information from in and around your body. For example, it instructs your body to grow and your **muscles** to move your arms and legs. Using your brain, you also learn, think, and make decisions such as whether to go for a bike ride.

NONSTOP BRAIN

Your brain is working nonstop, even when you are asleep at night. For example, your brain instructs your **heart** to keep pumping and your **lungs** to keep breathing all the time. Nighttime is when your brain also sorts out memories of what you have experienced during the day. That is why you sometimes wake up remembering a jumble of images and events from a dream.

Nerve network

The brain cannot move around to collect information from the rest of the body. It relies on a network of **nerves** to carry information to it. Nerves are like narrow threads spreading throughout your body. The nerve network includes the **spinal cord** and the outer nerves.

At the center

Your spinal cord is a white, shiny nerve in your back. It is the biggest nerve in your body, measuring up to 0.75 inches (2 cm) thick and about 16 inches (40 cm) long in adults. All the nerves around your body connect with the spinal cord. It directs information speedily to and from the brain. The spinal cord and brain together make up your **central nervous system**.

When you feel something with your fingers, nerves carry information about it to and from your brain.

The outer limits

There are billions of nerves inside you. The tiniest nerves are found at the outer limits of your body, anywhere from the tips of your toes to the tips of your ears. They join together to form larger and larger nerves that run like flexible cables throughout your body. It is similar to the way tiny twigs are attached to small branches that are attached to bigger branches and the trunk of a tree. These nerves connect with the spinal cord at different points.

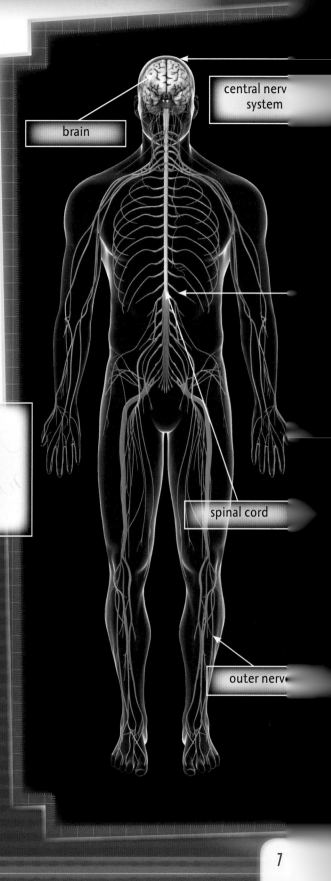

brain

central nerv
system

spinal cord

outer nerv

Nerves and the central nervous system work together to make a continuous pathway for information to and from all parts of the body.

SPINAL INJURIES

Sometimes people have bad accidents that injure their back or neck. If their spinal cord is broken or damaged, then it cannot carry all the usual information to and from the brain. People who have injured the middle of their spine may not be able to walk because information from the brain telling the legs to move cannot get to the leg nerves.

What Is the Brain Like?

The brain is a single body part that performs many important jobs. It has several different sections, and each section is responsible for different roles in the body.

Outside and in

Your brain looks pink, gray, and wrinkly on the outside. Inside it contains millions of nerve **cells**, called **neurons**. Cells are the building blocks of all parts of the human machine. The neurons together form nerve tissue. Tissues are groups of similar cells that work together. The brain is an **organ** made of different tissues that work together to do a job. For example, blood moves through blood vessel tissue to nerve tissue in the brain. It delivers the **oxygen** and nutrients brain cells need to release energy. This allows them to pass on, store, and process information properly.

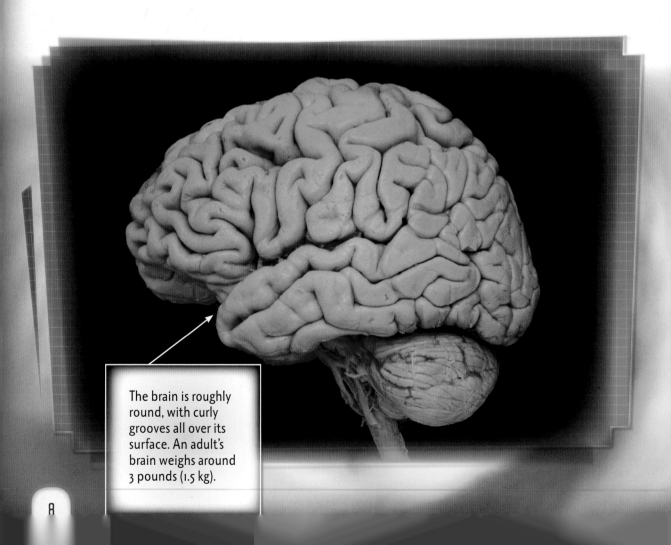

The brain is roughly round, with curly grooves all over its surface. An adult's brain weighs around 3 pounds (1.5 kg).

Protecting the brain

Without your brain you could not survive, so it is protected by special tissues. Your skull is a hard, bony case up to 0.5 inches (12 mm) thick that fits snugly around the brain. It protects the brain in the same way that the tough armor on a tank protects people inside. Between the skull and the brain are layers of tough tissue called the meninges. Fluid trapped between the meninges cushions the brain from knocking into the skull.

Drink plenty of water throughout the day to keep your brain fit.

WATER FOR THOUGHT

Brain surgeons say the living brain feels similar to the white of a boiled egg. It is soft and jelly-like because it is made mostly of watery fluid and fat. You cannot think as quickly as normal when you get thirsty. That is because your brain needs to add to the water in its fluid.

The largest part of the brain

Different parts of the brain's nerve tissue are responsible for different tasks. The **cerebrum** is the outermost and largest part of the brain. Its overall job is to allow us to respond to the world around us. The cerebrum has two halves, each made of four lobes, or parts. The lobe at the back controls vision. This means it makes sense of what your eyes detect. The lobe at the front controls speaking, thinking, and emotions such as feeling happy or sad. The other lobes control feelings, such as heat or pain, and hearing.

Beneath the cerebrum

Many other parts of the brain beneath the cerebrum take care of essential body maintenance. The **brain stem** controls essential activities such as breathing. It also makes us vomit unwanted substances from our stomachs. The cerebellum controls how you coordinate your movements, keep your balance, and stay upright.

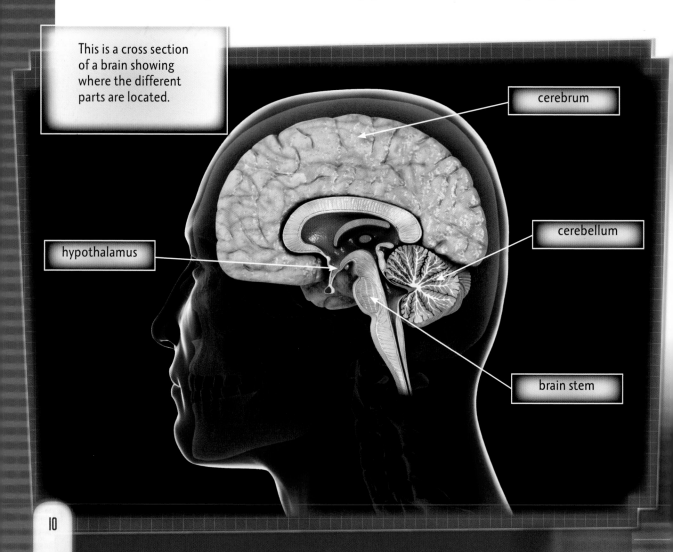

This is a cross section of a brain showing where the different parts are located.

cerebrum

cerebellum

hypothalamus

brain stem

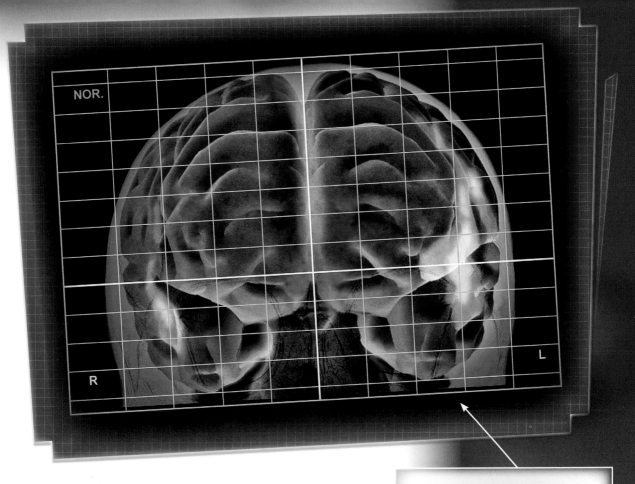

NOR.

R

L

The hypothalamus helps us to keep basic conditions in the body constant. We feel thirsty or hungry because the hypothalamus is processing information sent from different body parts that are starting to run out of water or food. The hypothalamus also helps us control our body temperature. This is essential to keeping our bodies working properly as well as making us feel sleepy.

This is a scan of the two frontal lobes. The orange and red areas show the parts of the lobe where most activity is taking place when someone is reading aloud.

POWER-HUNGRY MACHINE

The brain needs lots of energy to keep its different parts doing their jobs properly. It uses one-fifth of all the oxygen used by your body when you are at rest. It uses a smaller proportion when you are exercising because your muscles need lots of oxygen to keep them moving.

How Do Nerves Work?

Nerves carry messages rapidly between the nervous system and the rest of the body. They work because the neurons (nerve cells) they are made of are very good at passing on information.

Neurons

Nerves are made of bundles of long, thin threads of neurons arranged next to each other, like the links in a chain. The widest part of any neuron is the cell body. As in all other cells, this contains a mini-controller called a **nucleus** that keeps it alive. There are several **fibers** sprouting from the cell body. The longest fiber is called the **axon** and the shorter ones closest to the nucleus are called **dendrites**.

A nerve message, or **impulse**, travels in one direction through a neuron, from the cell body and along the axon. Impulses are like small bursts of electricity. A nerve bundle carries many impulses to and from different parts of the body.

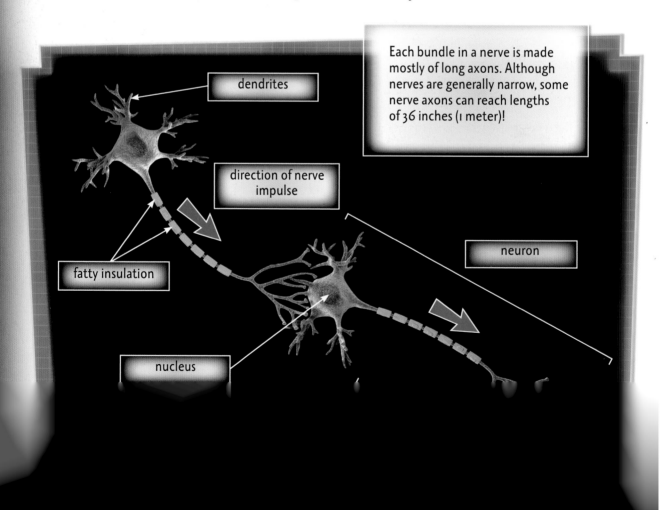

dendrites

direction of nerve impulse

Each bundle in a nerve is made mostly of long axons. Although nerves are generally narrow, some nerve axons can reach lengths of 36 inches (1 meter)!

neuron

fatty insulation

nucleus

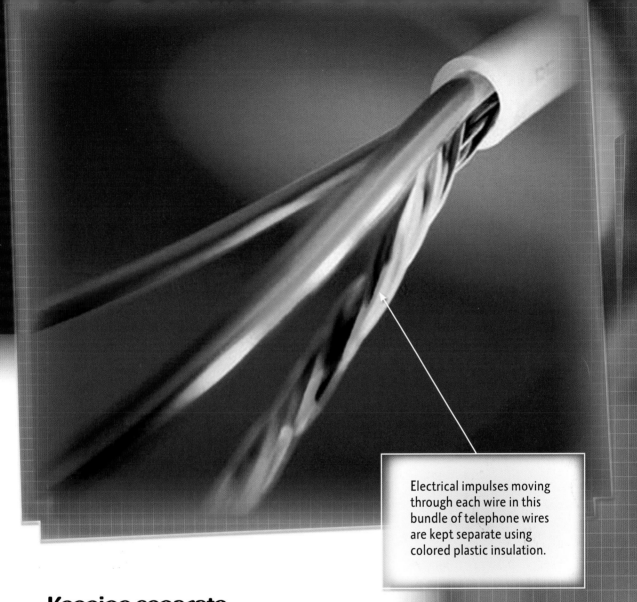

Electrical impulses moving through each wire in this bundle of telephone wires are kept separate using colored plastic insulation.

Keeping separate

Different threads in a nerve bundle carry separate impulses. Our bodies would not work properly if messages got lost or were sent to the wrong parts of the nervous system. The impulse is prevented from jumping from thread to thread by a fatty coating on the axons. The coating **insulates** the axon, similar to the way plastic insulates electrical wires.

DIFFERENT CELLS

All human cells, including neurons, wear out and die. Unlike other cells, our bodies cannot make new neurons to replace them. We can help to keep our neurons healthy and last longer by exercising them. So, stimulate your nervous system by trying out new tastes, sounds, and sights.

Passing it on

Impulses travel from neuron to neuron in a chain. They move from the longest fiber or axon of one neuron to the shortest fibers or dendrites of the next one. There are gaps between neurons called **synapses**. When an impulse arrives, chemicals are released from knobs at the end of an axon of one neuron. The chemicals move across the synapse and start an impulse off in the dendrite of the next neuron.

Neurons pass impulses to each other at speeds of up to 328 feet (100 meters) per second. That is far faster than sprinters in a relay race can pass on the baton!

PINS AND NEEDLES

Have you ever felt "pins and needles" in your feet after sitting in one position for a long time? Without knowing it, you were crushing the nerves in your feet. The feeling is caused by the neurons returning to normal and transmitting lots of messages again.

How Does the Brain Make Us React?

The brain responds to the information it receives. These responses are based partly on what we know through learning.

How to react

Impulses begin in **receptors**. These can be special cells or nerve fiber ends. When you touch an ice cube, the change in temperature in your finger makes a receptor under your skin create an impulse. The change in temperature is called a **stimulus**. Other stimuli that affect receptors in our bodies include bright light and sharp objects.

An impulse travels through **sensory neurons** to the part of the brain that can recognize the information. You then decide how to react. For example, you might want to move your finger from the ice cube when it feels numb. The brain starts off another impulse that moves through **motor neurons**. This impulse is a message telling how to react to the original stimulus, often by making muscles move.

The brain makes decisions based on stimuli from a lot of different sources.

Working automatically

Sometimes our brain reacts automatically, without us having to think about it. When we look at a bright light, the **pupils**, or openings, in our eyes get smaller. The brain does this to make sure that strong light does not damage sensitive tissues inside the eye. The parts of our nervous system that make our bodies react automatically without making decisions are together called the **autonomic nervous system**.

Our autonomic nervous system makes us salivate (drool) when we smell and see food. This prepares our bodies for digesting (breaking up) what we eat.

AT THE READY

If we are nervous or worried about something, our heart or breathing rate often gets faster. This is because the autonomic nervous system is getting our body ready in case we have to escape danger! Usually there is no real danger, and we can feel better simply by talking to other people.

Learning and memories

Have you learned how to swim? During lessons you will have gradually learned how to move your arms and legs in a way that lets you get through the water easily. At each lesson you remember what you learned in the previous lesson. Memories are records of information we have learned. Learning lets us develop new skills and remember or improve old ones. It helps us know what to do in the different situations we face in our lives.

How we learn

When an impulse passes through brain neurons, it causes a slight chemical change along that route for a fraction of a second. The brain automatically stores a record of the route for a short time. This is called a short-term memory. An example is a cell phone number we overhear a person giving to someone else. After about a minute we forget the information, unless we make an effort to memorize it. Your brain memorizes things by repeating the routes of impulses.

Our brain creates records of muscle movements and sounds when we learn how to play an instrument.

Making memories last

We usually forget unimportant information such as what we had for dinner or what was on TV a few days ago. However, we can remember some information, such as our birthday or when we broke our arm, for years and maybe all of our lives. Short-term memories turn into long-term memories when what we learn is important, significant, or useful to us.

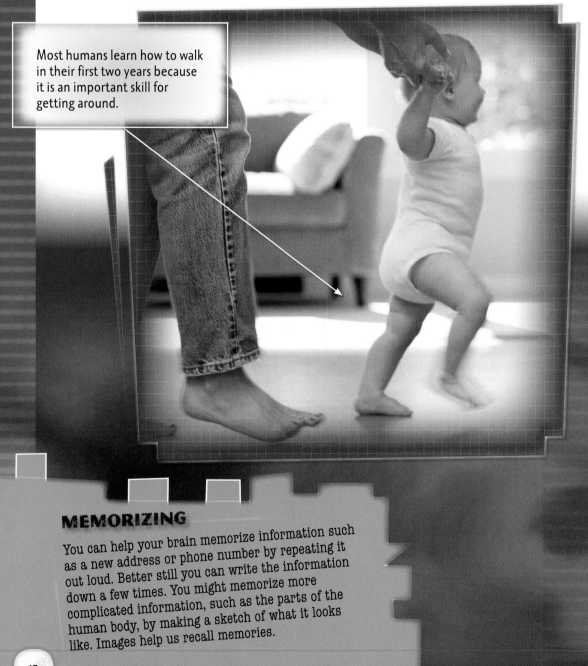

Most humans learn how to walk in their first two years because it is an important skill for getting around.

MEMORIZING

You can help your brain memorize information such as a new address or phone number by repeating it out loud. Better still you can write the information down a few times. You might memorize more complicated information, such as the parts of the human body, by making a sketch of what it looks like. Images help us recall memories.

What Are Reflexes?

The human machine can react to some stimuli very quickly without the brain getting involved. These reactions are called **reflexes**. Reflexes include pulling your hand away from something sharp and blinking when something moves toward your eyes. Reflexes happen so that the body can protect itself fast.

No-brainer

During a reflex the spinal cord acts as controller rather than the brain. A stimulus makes receptors start an impulse that travels through sensory neurons into the spinal cord. When the stimulus is a possible danger, special neurons in the cord directly connect sensory neurons with motor neurons. The impulse loops back to operate muscles that make the body avoid the danger. By not involving the brain, the reaction is almost immediate. Reflexes happen as part of the autonomic nervous system.

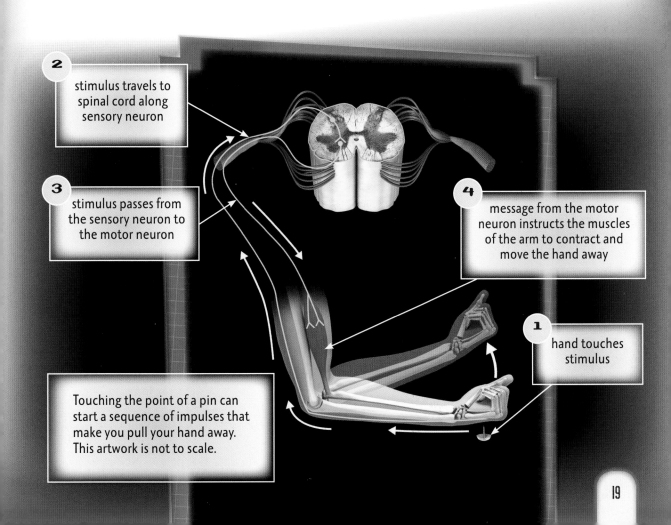

2 stimulus travels to spinal cord along sensory neuron

3 stimulus passes from the sensory neuron to the motor neuron

4 message from the motor neuron instructs the muscles of the arm to contract and move the hand away

1 hand touches stimulus

Touching the point of a pin can start a sequence of impulses that make you pull your hand away. This artwork is not to scale.

Reflex test

Doctors sometimes do the knee-jerk reflex test on people to check that their nervous system is working properly. You often sit with both legs dangling off the table while the doctor taps below your kneecap. This makes the spinal cord instruct your leg muscles to contract. The contraction of the muscle causes your lower leg to kick out. This reflex helps you keep your balance and stay standing if your leg is knocked, so you do not get injured.

REFLEXES FROM BIRTH

We develop some reflexes, such as avoiding hot things, as we grow up, but babies are born with several reflexes. One of these is a flap in their throat that automatically closes when they go underwater. This stops water from flooding their lungs. Others include suckling and grasping things that touch their palms. All of these reflexes can help them survive.

For some people it takes a few taps for sense receptors in the knee to start the reflex.

How Do Our Senses Work?

All the information you receive about everything outside your body comes from the five main **senses**. These are touching, seeing, hearing, smelling, and tasting. All except for touch rely on specialized sense organs—the eyes, ears, nose, and tongue.

Touch

The sense of touch tells you about the texture and feel of things around you. Touch receptors are all over our bodies in our skin, but there are lots grouped together in the fingers, lips, tongue, and soles of the feet. Some receptors are stimulated by slight pushes or pulls, others by larger changes.

Like a touch screen, your body reacts to slight pushes from other things that it touches.

READING TEXTURES

Braille is a reading system for blind people that uses the sense of touch. Different letters, words, and sentences are represented by different patterns of raised dots on paper. People run their fingertips over the paper to read.

Sight

The eyes are sense organs that let a person see. Light from the object you are looking at goes in through the pupil through a clear lens inside. The lens directs the light onto the **retina**. The retina is a tissue made of thousands of sensitive receptor cells. These cells can detect the brightness and color of light. Light stimuli make impulses move from each retinal cell toward the brain. They travel through a nerve called the optic nerve. Neurons in the cerebrum piece together the impulses into patterns of light. The brain sees images made up of these patterns.

In some ways, a digital camera is similar to an eye. Light enters the camera through a lens, although it hits a sensor rather than a retina. Tiny pixels, or squares, on the sensor detect light and send impulses to a microchip. The microchip processes and pieces together information into an image, or photo, that appears on a screen.

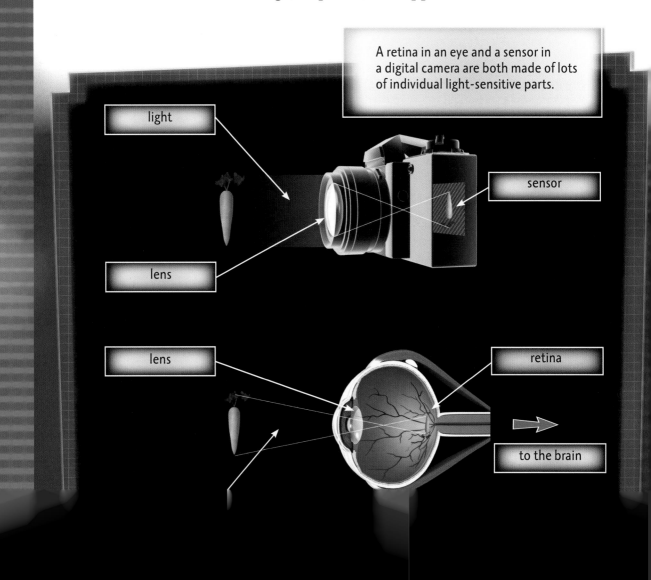

A retina in an eye and a sensor in a digital camera are both made of lots of individual light-sensitive parts.

light

sensor

lens

lens

retina

to the brain

Hearing

Sound is made when an object vibrates, or jiggles, back and forth. Vibrations make the air around the object move in ripples called sound waves. Sound waves enter your ear and hit a stretched tissue inside called the eardrum. This vibrates back and forth. The vibration is passed on to fluid in tubes deep inside the ear. Sound receptors lining the tubes create nerve impulses when the liquid moves past them. The brain converts the impulses into sounds.

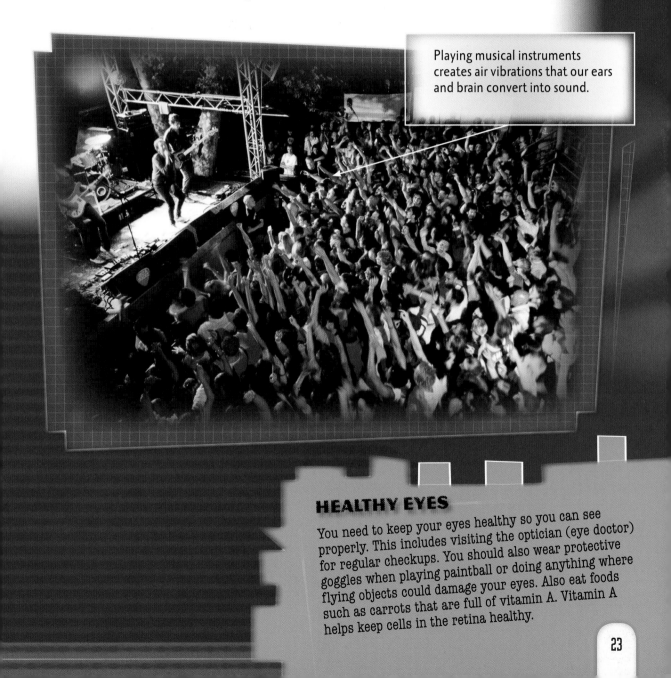

Playing musical instruments creates air vibrations that our ears and brain convert into sound.

HEALTHY EYES

You need to keep your eyes healthy so you can see properly. This includes visiting the optician (eye doctor) for regular checkups. You should also wear protective goggles when playing paintball or doing anything where flying objects could damage your eyes. Also eat foods such as carrots that are full of vitamin A. Vitamin A helps keep cells in the retina healthy.

Smell

The nose is a sense organ for detecting smells. There are over 10 million smell receptors lining the upper part of the inside of your nose. You smell chocolate, for example, when you breathe in tiny pieces of chocolate that have gotten into the air. Chemicals in the pieces dissolve into the mucus in the nose and stimulate some of the smell receptors. Your brain recognizes the pattern of impulses made by the receptors as a particular smell.

Perfume-makers train their sense of smell to distinguish and recognize hundreds of subtly different scents. They use their ability to invent new perfumes.

Taste

We sense the chemicals in food in our mouths using receptors called taste buds. These tiny organs are raised knobs or sunken pits. Most are on our tongues, but there are also receptors on the roof of the mouth. The effect of the chemicals on the buds stimulates a taste impulse. Each bud can only detect four tastes found in different foods. These are sweet, salty, sour (such as lemon juice), or bitter (such as coffee). All taste buds can detect these four tastes.

We can recognize many different flavors in food, from strawberries to cheese. Food chemicals stimulate not just taste buds but also smell receptors. We also sense the feel of food, such as its softness or temperature, using other receptors in our mouth.

This is a magnified photo of a taste bud on a tongue. Taste buds react to chemicals in food to produce taste.

CHANGING TASTES

When you are born you have about 10,000 taste buds. As you get older, taste buds die and are not replaced, so an adult may have only half as many taste buds as you do. That is why some foods may taste stronger to you than they do to an adult.

Caring for Your Control Center

To keep a machine like a computer working at its best, you need to take care of it and keep updating its software. The brain and nervous system in a human machine need similar care so that they work as well as they can.

Active mind

Keeping your mind active helps your brain store and retrieve information more easily. You can exercise your brain by doing crossword puzzles or sudoku or learning something new, such as juggling. Playing a musical instrument helps coordination and develops listening and counting skills.

Active body

Exercising your body is important, too. When you are active, you breathe harder and faster. This brings more oxygen into the brain, which makes it release the energy it needs. Exercise also makes the brain release chemicals called endorphins that make us feel good. The brain has the natural protection of the skull, but you should still be careful to avoid brain injuries. One way to do this is to wear a helmet when cycling.

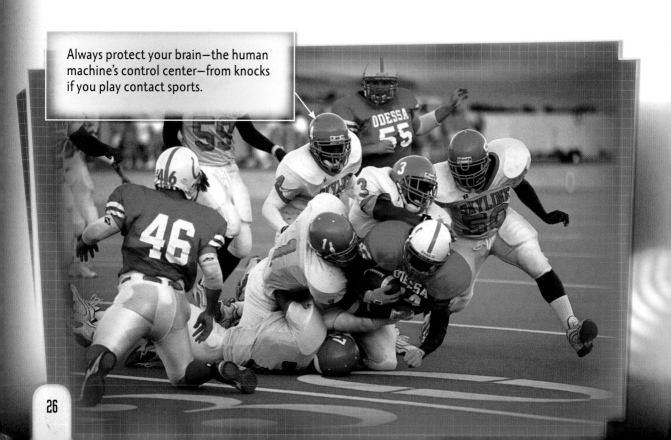

Always protect your brain—the human machine's control center—from knocks if you play contact sports.

Try to eat a mix of foods at breakfast. Carbohydrates such as oats are good for energy, fruit juice gives you vitamins, and eggs or milk provide protein.

Eating well

Your whole body needs a regular supply of healthy fuel, but breakfast is especially important. Eating a healthy breakfast will give your body energy to keep your brain working all morning. Some foods are also known to be good for the brain and nervous system. Eggs help make healthy synapses (the connecting points between neurons), and the fats found in oily fish can keep neurons healthy.

ARE YOU GETTING ENOUGH SLEEP?

It is good to be active, but do not forget that your brain and body also need rest. On average a teenager needs nine hours of sleep, although some will sleep as much as twelve or as little as four hours a night. It all depends on the individual!

The World's Most Complex Machine

The human body is often described as the world's most complex machine, but of course it is not really a machine at all. Machines are non-living, mechanical objects, whereas our bodies are natural, living things. But there are similarities. Like a machine, the body is made up of different parts that work together in systems to do particular jobs. These different systems work together to make the whole body— or the human machine—run smoothly and efficiently.

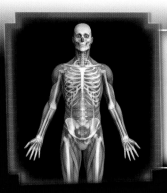

THE SKELETAL SYSTEM

This system of bones supports the other parts of the body, rather like the way the metal frame of a car supports the vehicle.

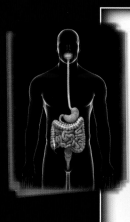

THE DIGESTIVE SYSTEM

The digestive system works as a food-processing machine. It consists of various organs that work together to break down food into forms that the body can use as fuel and raw materials.

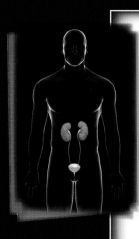

THE EXCRETORY SYSTEM

This is the human machine's waste disposal system, removing harmful substances and waste produced by the other parts of the body.

THE NERVOUS SYSTEM

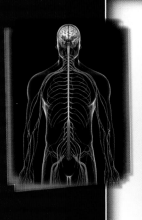

This is the human machine's communication and control system. The brain transmits and receives messages from the senses and the rest of the body. It does this through a network of nerves connected to the brain via the spinal cord.

THE CIRCULATORY SYSTEM

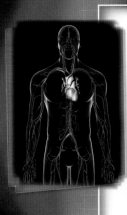

This is the body's delivery system. The heart pumps blood through blood vessels, carrying nutrients and oxygen to the other parts and removing waste from cells.

THE RESPIRATORY SYSTEM

This system provides the rest of the body with the oxygen it needs to get energy from food. It also releases waste gases from the body into the air.

THE MUSCULAR SYSTEM

Muscles are the human machine's motors. Some muscles make the bones of the skeleton move, while others work as pumps to keep substances moving through the body.

Glossary

autonomic nervous system part of the nervous system that controls important bodily functions without the brain making a decision to do so, such as sweating during exercise

axon longest fiber of a neuron

brain stem part of the brain closest to the spinal cord that controls essential activity such as breathing

cell building block of all living things. The human body is made up of millions of different cells.

central nervous system brain and spinal cord

cerebrum largest, upper part of the brain that controls speech, coordination, memory, and other functions

dendrite shortest fibers from the cell body of a neuron

fiber thin strand

heart muscular organ that pumps blood throughout the body

impulse electrical signal that travels along a nerve

insulate cover something so that it does not lose energy

lungs organs that we use to breathe. The lungs are part of the body's respiratory system.

motor neuron nerve cell that carries impulses from the brain and spinal cord to muscles

muscle tissue in the body that contracts (tightens) to cause movement

nerve groups of neurons. Nerves pass information to and from the brain and the rest of the body.

neuron bundle of fibers that carries messages between the brain and the rest of the body

nucleus control center in a cell

organ part of the body that performs a specific function, such as the heart or brain

oxygen gas in the air

pupil hole in the middle of the iris in the eye

receptor cell, tissue, or organ that creates impulses when stimulated

reflex fast reaction controlled by the spinal cord

retina layer in the back of the eye that senses light and transmits impulses through the optic nerve to the brain

senses how the body feels anything around it. The five senses are sight, hearing, touch, smell, and taste.

sensory neuron nerve cells that carry impulses from sense receptors to the central nervous system

spinal cord bundle of nerves inside the spine, which runs from the brain down the length of the back

stimulus (plural is **stimuli**) something that triggers an impulse in a receptor that moves into nerves

synapse connecting point between neurons. An impulse crosses a synapse when it is transmitted from one neuron to another.

Find Out More

Websites

"The Brain is the Boss" at www.kidshealth.org/kid/body/brain_noSW.html has more details about what the parts of the brain do and how it connects with nerves. The "KidsHealth" website also has sections on all parts of our bodies.

At http://insideout.rigb.org/insideout/anatomy/tissue_issues/nerves.html you can find out more about nerves and even play a game called "Nerve wrecker"!

At http://yucky.discovery.com/noflash/body/pg000142.html you will learn more about eyes. Other pages on this body site have information about the nervous system and the brain.

At www.exploratorium.edu/memory/index.html you can exercise your brain by playing memory games.

Books

Funston, Sylvia. *It's All in Your Head: A Guide to Your Brilliant Brain.* Toronto, Ont.: Maple Tree, 2005.

Green, Jen. *Brain and Senses.* Mankato, Minn.: Stargazer, 2005.

Sousa, David A. *Brain-Compatible Activities.* Thousand Oaks, Calif.: Corwin, 2007.

Walker, Richard. *Human Body.* New York: Dorling Kindersley, 2006.

Index